UNDERSTANDING

TRANSCRANIAL MAGNETIC STIMULATION

Mastering The Art Of Science For Emerging Trends For Optimal Brain Health, Potential Benefits, Therapies Applications And More

DR. KARSON BRYAN

Copyright © 2023, Dr. Karson Bryan

DISCLAIMER

This book's content is meant to be used solely for general informative purposes. Despite having taken every precaution to guarantee the content's accuracy, the author disclaims all duty and responsibility for any errors or omissions. It is recommended that readers exercise caution and, if needed, seek expert guidance. Any and all liability for losses, damages, or other outcomes arising from the use of the material included in this book is disclaimed by the author and publisher. All referenced product names and trademarks are the property of their respective owners and are merely cited for identification. Any likeness to real people or things is entirely accidental. Since it is a work of fiction, this book should not be used as a substitute for professional, legal, or medical advice. It is advised that readers seek advice on particular issues from qualified experts."

Please make sure that this disclaimer is modified to fit the particular requirements and subject matter of your book. Seeking advice from a legal expert is also a smart option if you have any questions or require a more thorough disclaimer for your specific book.

TABLE OF CONTENTS

CHAPTER ONE

TRANSCRANIAL MAGNETIC STIMULATION

INTRODUCTION

TRANSCRANIAL MAGNETIC STIMULATION: WHAT IS IT?

The non-invasive neurostimulation method known as transcranial magnetic stimulation (TMS) has drawn a lot of interest from the fields of clinical psychiatry and neuroscience. TMS is a useful tool for both research and therapeutic purposes since it uses magnetic fields to induce electrical currents that activate particular brain areas. This introduction will give a thorough overview of TMS, covering its foundational ideas, historical background, and current relevance in the fields of clinical and neurological medicine.

AN OVERVIEW OF TMS'S HISTORY

TMS's origins can be traced back to British scientist Michael Faraday's discovery of electromagnetic induction in the late 1700s. The foundation for comprehending the relationship between magnetic fields and electrical currents was established by Faraday's groundbreaking research. But it wasn't until the latter half of the 20th century that these ideas were applied to the non-invasive stimulation of the human brain.

When Anthony Barker and associates created the first working TMS device that could stimulate the human brain in the 1980s, the modern era of TMS officially began. Their research represented a critical turning point in neuroscience by enabling hitherto unattainable studies of brain connection and function. This cutting-edge technology quickly proved to be an invaluable resource for learning about the complex neural networks that underpin different cognitive and motor skills as well as for researching brain physiology.

TMS's non-invasiveness is one of its main benefits. Unlike conventional techniques, which necessitate electrode implantation or surgical procedures, TMS targets specific brain regions with targeted magnetic pulses delivered from outside the skull. This feature of TMS has made it a significant tool for studying brain illness and function since it enables researchers to look into the neuronal circuits underlying different motor, emotional, and cognitive activities.

Furthermore, TMS is now widely used in the field of clinical psychiatry. Treatments for depression, anxiety disorders, and some neurological diseases including Parkinson's disease are among its medicinal uses. In particular, repetitive transcranial magnetic stimulation (RTMS) has drawn interest because it may be able to help individuals with depression who are resistant to conventional treatments by reducing symptoms.

Recent developments in TMS technology include neuronavigation systems, which improve stimulation precision and allow physicians and researchers to more precisely target particular brain regions. TMS has been shown to have the potential to treat addiction as well as improve cognition and help people recover from brain injuries. This research is still in progress.

Transcranial magnetic stimulation is a major advancement in clinical psychiatry and neuroscience. Its historical development which has its roots in Faraday's groundbreaking work and later advances in the late 20th century has opened the door to a greater comprehension of brain function as well as a variety of therapeutic applications. TMS is a highly adaptable technique that has the potential to transform both the treatment of many neurological and psychiatric problems as well as our understanding of the human brain. This is due to its non-invasive nature and ability to target specific brain regions.

CHAPTER TWO

THE BASIS OF TMS INTERVENTION

THE BASICS OF BRAIN FUNCTION

Our neurological system, which governs our thoughts, feelings, movements, and physical processes, is centered on the human brain, an astonishingly intricate and complex organ. The essential components of the nervous system, billions of neurons, interact with one another to power the brain's basic operations. Through an extensive network of connections known as synapses, these neurons can exchange information and transmit electrical signals to one another. This complex network of synapses and neurons is the basis of all behavioral and cognitive functions.

UNDERSTANDING SYNAPSES AND NEURONS

The basic structural and functional elements of the nervous system are composed of specialized cells called neurons. Despite their diverse forms and dimensions, they all serve the same fundamental purpose, which is the transmission of electrochemical impulses. An axon, dendrites, and cell body make up a neuron. While the axon sends information to other neurons or effectors cells, such as muscles or glands, dendrites receive incoming signals from other neurons. A synapse is the point of interaction where two neurons connect and exchange information.

Neurons cannot communicate without synapses. The release of neurotransmitters occurs in the synaptic cleft, a tiny space between the transmitting and receiving neurons when an electrical impulse known as an action potential passes through one neuron's axon and reaches the synapse.

The signal spreads when these neurotransmitters attach to receptors on the dendrites of the receiving neuron. A crucial component of learning and memory is the ability to change the effectiveness and strength of synaptic connections, a process known as synaptic plasticity.

BRAIN AREAS AND FUNCTIONS

The brain is divided into various areas, each of which is in charge of carrying out particular tasks. While our knowledge of the intricate workings of the brain is still developing, several general classifications of brain regions and their roles have been established. Thinking, reasoning, and conscious awareness are examples of higher-order cognitive processes that are controlled by the cerebral cortex. While the brainstem is in charge of basic life-sustaining processes like breathing and heart rate regulation, the limbic system is heavily involved in emotions and memory formation.

NEUROPLASTICITY AND LEARNING

Also known as brain plasticity, neuroplasticity refers to the brain's amazing capacity to change and rearrange itself throughout an individual's lifetime. It is the cornerstone of memory and learning. Our brains undergo structural and functional changes at both the synaptic and neuronal levels when we pick up new knowledge or skills.

This adaptation may entail the development of new neurons as well as the strengthening or weakening of synaptic connections, especially in the hippocampus, a region crucial to memory.

The brain's capacity to heal from wounds, adjusts to new situations, and maximizes its performance all stem from neuroplasticity. This phenomenon emphasizes how crucial it is to continue learning throughout life and partake in mentally taxing activities to preserve cognitive function and vigor.

PRINCIPLES OF MAGNETIC STIMULATION

Using electromagnetic fields to affect neural activity in certain brain regions, Transcranial Magnetic Stimulation (TMS) is a non-invasive neuromodulation therapy. It is based on the electromagnetic induction concept, according to which magnetic fields that change quickly cause electrical currents to flow through adjacent brain tissue.

TMS has been used in several therapeutic settings, including the management of anxiety, depression, and a few neurological conditions.

Targeted magnetic pulses are delivered to particular brain regions via a magnetic coil applied to the scalp in the basic idea of TMS. Depending on the settings, these pulses can either stimulate or inhibit neural activity. TMS can modify neuroplasticity, which may be advantageous for research and therapeutic applications like brain function mapping and examining the underlying causes of different neurological and psychiatric disorders. Advances in TMS therapy could lead to new therapeutic approaches and a better knowledge of the human brain.

CHAPTER THREE

MAGNETIC FIELDS AND ELECTROMAGNETIC FIELDS

CREATING A BRAIN ELECTRIC CURRENT

A powerful magnetic field is applied to the human brain during transcranial magnetic stimulation (TMS), a non-invasive neurostimulation method. This magnetic field causes an electric current to flow through the neural tissue, which depolarizes neurons and changes brain activity as a result. TMS has drawn a lot of interest because of its capacity to examine and modify brain neural circuits in both clinical and scientific contexts.

TMS DEVICE TYPES

TMS devices come in a variety of forms, each with unique features and uses. The most often used TMS devices are circular and figure-of-eight coils, which provide broad and targeted stimulation zones, respectively. While circular coils are utilized for more diffuse and broader stimulation, figure-of-eight coils are commonly used for precision targeting of particular brain areas. Apart from these, there are also specific TMS devices like repetitive TMS (RTMS) and deep TMS (DTMS), which are intended to be applied to repeat magnetic stimulation pulses for therapeutic purposes or to access deeper brain areas.

THE TMS'S MECHANISMS

The electromagnetic induction equation of Faraday is crucial to the TMS's basic working principle. An electric field is induced within the brain tissue when a magnetic field is rapidly modified, as happens when a TMS coil is powered with a high-intensity electrical pulse. Neurons in the stimulated area get activated as a result of this electric field. Since neurons are excitable cells, the produced electric field can depolarize their membrane potential, which can start action potentials and change neuronal activity. Though the precise processes by which TMS alters brain activity are still being studied, modifications to neurotransmitter release and synaptic plasticity are thought to be involved.

ACTIVATING BRAIN FUNCTION

Depending on the stimulation parameters, TMS can be used to either stimulate or inhibit neuronal activity. Researchers can study the function of a specific brain region by applying a single TMS pulse to that location, which can temporarily excite the neurons in that area. On the other hand, TMS can either increase or decrease neuronal activity when it is given repetitively at a specific frequency (RTMS). This has significant implications for clinical applications like the treatment of depression. Brain-behavior connections and functional brain connectivity mapping are further applications of TMS.

BOTH IMMEDIATE AND LONG-TERM EFFECTS

TMS affects the brain in the short and maybe long term. Neural activity in the stimulated region is altered as one of the initial impacts of TMS, and this effect might persist for a few seconds to several minutes following stimulation. On the other hand, longer-lasting alterations in brain function might result from repeated or protracted TMS sessions, as in the case of RTMS for depression. Changes in neurogenesis, neurotransmitter levels, and synaptic plasticity are thought to be the cause of these long-term consequences. Research is currently ongoing to determine the long-term effects' durability and clinical importance.

ELEMENTS AFFECTING TMS PERFORMANCE

Numerous factors, including as the stimulation parameters, coil design, and specific features of the person, affect the effectiveness of TMS. The strength, frequency, and duration of TMS are examples of stimulation characteristics that are critical in determining the results.

The spatial specificity of the stimulation is influenced by the coil design, including its shape and orientation. Furthermore, the effectiveness of TMS can be greatly impacted by individual factors, such as the subject's neural network status and the placement of the targeted brain area. Individual differences in TMS responses can also be attributed to genetics, age, and the existence of neurological or psychiatric disorders.

Transcranial magnetic stimulation is a flexible and promising method for monitoring and adjusting brain activity.

Researchers and clinicians looking to maximize the potential of TMS in the disciplines of neuroscience and neuromodulation must have a thorough understanding of the different kinds of

TMS devices, the mechanisms behind TMS, its effects on neural activity, and the factors influencing its efficacy. TMS is still advancing our understanding of the brain and has enormous potential for treating a range of neurological and psychiatric conditions.

CHAPTER FOUR

TMS'S CLINICAL APPLICATIONS

USES IN DIAGNOSIS AND TREATMENT

Clinical neuroscience has given considerable attention to transcranial magnetic stimulation (TMS) due to its dual use in therapeutic and diagnostic settings. Electromagnetic pulses are applied to the scalp during TMS, a non-invasive, painless procedure that can alter brain activity by interacting with underlying neural tissue. Its therapeutic uses target a range of neurological and psychiatric problems, while its diagnostic applications center on investigating brain activity and connectivity.

MAKING BRAIN DISORDER DIAGNOSES

TMS provides a special view into how the brain functions in humans. It can be used to map the parts of the brain responsible for particular processes, such as memory, language, and motor control, for diagnostic purposes. For instance, motor cortex mapping using TMS can assist in the diagnosis of motor diseases by identifying the cortical representation of muscles. Beyond this, TMS may be used to evaluate the structural integrity of cerebral connections, which makes it an invaluable diagnostic and understanding tool for diseases like multiple sclerosis and stroke. In addition, TMS application during neuroimaging allows researchers to explore the causal linkages between particular brain regions and cognitive functions, improving our understanding of conditions such as epilepsy and Alzheimer's disease.

APPLICATIONS OF THERAPEUTICS IN MENTAL HEALTH

TMS has become known as a promising therapy method in the field of mental health. The treatment of depression is one of the most noteworthy uses. Major Depressive Disorder (MDD) is a common, crippling illness that frequently responds poorly to conventional therapies including medication and psychotherapy. Since TMS can affect the activity of important brain regions linked to mood regulation, it provides an alternative for those with depression who are not responding to medication. The FDA has approved repetitive TMS (RTMS) of the dorsolateral prefrontal cortex as a treatment option for MDD, indicating that it may help patients with the condition's symptoms and enhance their quality of life.

DEVELOPING THERAPEUTIC USES

Novel clinical uses for a range of neurological and psychiatric diseases are developing as TMS research continues to progress. Notably, the potential of TMS in anxiety disorders is being investigated. The brain regions responsible for anxiety disorders, such as the prefrontal cortex and amygdala, exhibit dysregulated activity. These disorders include social anxiety disorder and generalized anxiety disorder. Targeting these regions with TMS therapies aims to improve general functioning and reduce symptoms of anxiety.

TMS IN ANXIETY AND DEPRESSION

TMS has demonstrated impressive success when used to treat depression. High-frequency repetitive TMS has been used to excite the prefrontal cortex and reestablish the neuronal balance related to mood regulation. Over many weeks, the technique entails daily sessions, and clinical trials have shown a considerable improvement in depression symptoms.

TMS is also used to treat anxiety problems. Early research in this field has demonstrated promise in lowering symptoms of anxiety, even if the field is still developing. The amygdala is a crucial component linked to anxiety reactions, and its hyperactivity can be modulated by applying TMS to the prefrontal cortex. This approach has the potential to be a non-pharmacological therapy alternative and is less intrusive than surgical procedures.

TMS has established a position for itself in the diagnosis and treatment landscape of mental and neurological illnesses. Through its diagnostic applications, a deeper understanding of brain activity and connectivity is made possible, which helps with condition monitoring and diagnosis. For those in the mental health field who don't react well to conventional therapies, TMS provides a non-invasive and successful therapeutic method, especially in the treatment of depression and anxiety. With further research, TMS may find new uses in medicine, providing patients suffering from a variety of neurological and psychiatric disorders with hope.

CHAPTER FIVE

REALISTIC ASPECTS

A non-invasive medical technique called transcranial magnetic stimulation (TMS) is used to treat a range of neuropsychiatric illnesses, such as anxiety, depression, and specific neurological abnormalities. Even though TMS therapy can be a safe and successful treatment option for many people, it's important to know everything there is to know about the process, including related safety precautions and recommendations, before beginning TMS therapy. The main practical issues surrounding TMS will be discussed in this article, along with the technique itself, safety measures, possible side effects, and how to select a certified TMS provider.

TMS PROCEDURE AND SAFETY

Targeted magnetic pulses are delivered to particular brain regions using electromagnetic coils during the TMS procedure. These pulses cause electrical currents to flow across brain cells, modifying brain function and perhaps relieving symptoms related to several illnesses. In TMS, patient safety is the top priority, and stringent procedures are adhered to to guarantee their welfare. To reduce dangers, TMS must be administered by qualified specialists in a monitored medical setting.

GETTING READY FOR A TMS SESSION

It's important to talk to your TMS practitioner about your medical history and any current drugs before your TMS session. This data will guarantee your safety throughout the process and assist in determining the best treatment parameters. Although TMS is usually a well-tolerated treatment, making these preparations will allow the session to be customized to meet your specific needs.

The TMS Procedure: A specially designed coil is applied to your scalp while you are comfortably seated for a TMS session. Over 20 to 30 minutes, the practitioner will apply repeated magnetic pulses to the targeted area of your brain. You won't feel much discomfort throughout the treatment, and you'll stay awake the entire time. TMS treatments are usually given according to your condition and the treatment plan regularly, such as every day for a few weeks.

GUIDELINES AND SAFETY MEASURES:

TMS safety measures involve carefully assessing each person's unique needs for stimulation intensity, location, and duration. This is usually determined by the particular neuroanatomy and state of the patient. According to safety regulations, the process must also be closely watched to detect any negative consequences as soon as possible.

COMMON SIDE EFFECTS

TMS frequently causes minor, temporary side effects. During the treatment, they may include headaches, moderate scalp discomfort, and localized muscular contractions. As the course of the treatment progresses, these symptoms usually become less noticeable.

SEIZURE RISK AND SAFETY MEASURES

Although it is incredibly rare, one of the more serious concerns connected to TMS is the potential to cause a seizure. Practitioners adhere to established safety protocols to reduce this risk. These protocols include identifying the proper stimulation parameters, closely monitoring the patient throughout the session, and putting safety precautions in place, such as the ability to stop the procedure right away if any concerning signs appear.

SELECTING A TMS PROVIDER

Selecting a trustworthy and qualified provider is crucial when thinking about TMS therapy. Here are some important things to think about:

Locating a Certified Professional:

1. Credentials: Verify that the TMS practitioner has received specialized training in TMS therapy and is a licensed medical professional, such as a neurologist or psychiatrist.

2. Expertise: Seek a practitioner who has successfully treated patients in the past and has a great deal of expertise in delivering TMS.

3. Accreditation: Confirm that the TMS therapy facility is accredited and upholds quality and safety requirements.

4. Patient Reviews: To learn more about the satisfaction and experiences of past patients, look for patient reviews and testimonials.

TMS is a potentially effective treatment for a range of neuropsychiatric conditions. It is important to choose a skilled practitioner and to be well-informed about the technique, safety precautions, and potential adverse effects. To find out if TMS is the best course of action for your problem and to guarantee your safety during therapy, you should always speak with a medical expert.

CHAPTER SIX

TECHNOLOGICAL PROGRESS IN TMS

HIGH-PERFORMANCE TMS

Technological developments in Transcranial Magnetic Stimulation (TMS) have completely changed the fields of neuropsychiatry and neuroscience. These developments have paved the way for more effective treatment options, deeper comprehension of how the brain works, and investigation of cutting-edge uses. Among these incredible developments is High-Frequency TMS. With high-frequency TMS, quick magnetic pulses—typically at frequencies higher than 5 Hz—are used to stimulate the brain. This method has drawn interest because it may be able to modulate brain activity more successfully than traditional TMS, which makes it useful in a range of therapeutic and research contexts. Targeting certain brain regions, high-frequency TMS is being studied for its potential to enhance neuronal plasticity and help cure disorders including addiction, depression, and chronic pain.

BURST STIMULATION THETA

In TMS technology, Theta Burst Stimulation (TBS) is another noteworthy advancement. To cause long-term depression (LTD) or long-term potentiation (LTP) in the targeted brain region, TBS uses a certain pattern of repeating magnetic pulses. TBS has the potential to be employed therapeutically in neurological rehabilitation and cognitive enhancement by modulating two essential processes involved in learning and memory: LTD and LTP.

TWO-PULSE TMS

The technique known as Paired-Pulse TMS entails rapidly delivering two magnetic pulses with different intervals between them. With the use of this technique, scientists can investigate the relationships between various brain regions and the temporal dynamics of neural circuits. Paired-pulse TMS has significant implications for neural network mapping and has been essential in helping to understand the connectivity and functional interactions between different brain areas.

TMS IN DEVELOPMENT AND RESEARCH

TMS has become widely used in research and development because it offers a non-invasive way to look into the composition and operation of the brain. TMS is a tool used by researchers to investigate the neurological underpinnings of a variety of cognitive functions, including perception, attention, memory, and decision-making. TMS also plays a key role in investigating the neurological underpinnings of psychiatric diseases and assessing the effectiveness of possible therapies.

IMPROVING COGNITIVE FUNCTION

TMS is essential to the fascinating topic of cognitive improvement, which has attracted a lot of interest lately. Targeting particular brain regions implicated in cognitive functioning, transcranial magnetic stimulation (TMS) has demonstrated the potential to improve cognition, memory, and decision-making. These developments help patients with neurological conditions-related cognitive impairments as well as healthy people wishing to improve their cognitive function.

UTILIZATION FOR RESEARCH IN PSYCHIATRY

The field of TMS investigational uses in psychiatry is growing quickly. Numerous psychiatric conditions, including major depressive disorder, schizophrenia, bipolar disorder, and obsessive-compulsive disorder, are being investigated as potential treatments with TMS. TMS has potential benefits over conventional therapy due to its non-invasive nature and capacity to target specific brain regions, especially for patients who do not respond well to conventional medicines.

REGULATORY AND ETHICAL CONSIDERATIONS

Regulation and ethical issues are crucial to TMS technology development. To protect patient safety and the responsible use of TMS, it is essential to create ethical guidelines and regulatory frameworks as the technology becomes more widely available and is employed in a variety of clinical and research settings. Concerns about informed consent, possible hazards, and fair access to TMS treatments are examples of ethical dilemmas.

PERSONALIZED MEDICINE AND TMS

Additionally, TMS is essential to the developing field of personalized medicine. Neuroimaging and neurophysiological data are used to determine the precise brain regions and circuits that require modulation for each patient, allowing TMS treatment to be customized for them. A more focused and efficient method of treating mental illnesses is made possible by the exciting development of precision psychiatry. This method seeks to maximize treatment results by tailoring the appropriate TMS procedure to each patient's distinct neural profile.

Developments in TMS technology, such as paired-pulse TMS, high-frequency TMS, Theta Burst Stimulation, and the investigation of TMS in research and development have the potential to fundamentally alter our comprehension of the brain and revolutionize the management of neurological and psychiatric disorders. In addition to these technological developments, ethical and legal issues must be taken into account.

CHAPTER SEVEN

OPPORTUNITIES AND DIFFICULTIES

PROSPECTS FOR TMS THERAPY IN THE FUTURE

The field of neurological and mental health therapies has evolved with the introduction of transcranial magnetic stimulation (TMS) therapy. There are several intriguing paths that TMS therapy is likely to go in the future. Refinement of TMS technology and approaches is one of the most promising elements. Scientists and medical professionals are always looking for ways to better target particular brain regions and customize treatments for each patient to increase the accuracy and efficacy of TMS. By becoming more customized, therapy results can be increased and adverse effects can be decreased.

Furthermore, there's a rising interest in investigating TMS's potential use for treating a larger spectrum of neurological and psychiatric disorders. Current studies are looking into TMS's potential advantages for problems like PTSD, addiction, and even neurodegenerative disorders like Parkinson's and Alzheimer's disease. TMS has previously demonstrated success in treating depression and several anxiety disorders. These investigations may greatly broaden the application of TMS therapy.

The creation of new TMS modalities and equipment is a noteworthy path for the future of TMS therapy. Researchers are developing novel ideas to improve treatment accessibility and convenience, such as portable TMS devices that patients can use at home. TMS's therapeutic potential is also being further enhanced by the increased availability of real-time, feedback-driven therapies made possible by developments in brain imaging and neurophysiological monitoring.

POSSIBLE INNOVATIONS

There are several possible developments in TMS therapy that could revolutionize the way we treat neurological and mental health conditions. TMS protocol optimization is one fascinating field of study. To improve treatment strategies, scientists are experimenting with several stimulation settings, including frequency, intensity, and duration. This may result in even more potent and efficient treatments, possibly with shorter course lengths and better results for patients.

Combining TMS with various therapeutic techniques is another promising topic. Combining TMS with psychotherapy or pharmaceutical therapies may have synergistic benefits that give patients with complicated diseases additional all-encompassing therapeutic alternatives. The way we treat mental health illnesses could be completely changed by this multimodal strategy.

Furthermore, as our knowledge of the neuroplasticity of the brain and its significance for mental health expands, TMS therapy may find new uses. Customizing TMS to target particular neurological elements that underlie disorders like anxiety or depression could lead to advancements in precision medicine and more efficient therapeutic approaches.

TMS AND THE STATE OF HEALTHCARE

TMS therapy is progressively making its way into the larger healthcare system, and there are opportunities and obstacles associated with its integration. The need for greater understanding and acceptance within the medical community is one of the main obstacles. TMS is still relatively new, thus efforts to enlighten and educate healthcare providers about its uses and advantages will be essential to its broader acceptance.

Positively, TMS may become more widely recognized in mainstream healthcare as a result of the increased awareness of the significance of mental health and brain-related diseases. With the prevalence of mental health disorders rising, TMS can supplement or replace conventional treatments in a non-invasive and generally safe manner. Patients pursuing TMS therapy may have more insurance coverage and accessibility as a result of this growing acceptance.

Moreover, TMS may help close the knowledge gap between neurology and mental health. There are neurobiological commonalities between many psychiatric and neurological conditions, and TMS can be a therapeutic approach that unifies these conditions. Including TMS in all-encompassing treatment plans that address neurological and psychiatric issues could provide a more patient-centered approach to care.

There are a lot of exciting things that TMS therapy can do in the future, like improving precision and developing new treatment modalities or integrating it into the larger healthcare system. Although there are still obstacles to overcome, the potential advancements in TMS therapy have the potential to significantly improve the lives of people with a variety of neurological and mental health conditions. TMS has the potential to significantly change our understanding of and approach to treating these conditions as science and technology continue to progress.